Bikes

By M. J. Calabro

CELEBRATION PRESS
Pearson Learning Group

CONTENTS

Lance Armstrong

Thousands of people line the main street of Paris, France, on a summer day. The mood is festive. Many people wave American flags.

The spectators cheer wildly as a bicycle racer comes into view, pedals flying. His average racing speed is more than 25 miles per hour.

As the crowd roars, the rider, Lance Armstrong, crosses the finish line. This athlete from Texas has just won the Tour de France, a demanding road race. The 2003 Tour covered more than 2,000 miles, including steep mountain climbs. It lasted three weeks, with only two rest days.

Armstrong's 2003 triumph was amazing for many reasons. He had won the Tour de France for the fifth time in a row. In the history of the yearly event, which began in 1903, only four other riders won the Tour five times. Of those five-time winners, only one other rider ever won five years in a row. Most important to Armstrong, though, was the fact that he is the first cancer survivor to win the Tour de France.

In October 1996, Armstrong learned he had cancer. It spread to his lungs, abdomen, and brain. Doctors put his chances of survival at 40 percent. His racing team cancelled his contract.

Armstrong never doubted that he would live and race again. Medical treatments halted the cancer, and he began training again.

By 1998, Armstrong was back on the bike. He had been hired by a racing team sponsored by the U.S. Postal Service. As that team's lead rider, Armstrong began his string of Tour de France wins in 1999. He also competed in the 2000 Olympic Games, winning a bronze medal.

Armstrong plans to keep racing in the Tour de France. He wants to become the first six-time winner. Along with training and racing, he raises money for cancer research.

Lance Armstrong rode the first American-made bicycle ever to win the Tour de France.

Armstrong's bicycle is an amazing machine that represents more than 100 years of progress in bike technology. The frame is a composite of carbon fiber and a special kind of glue. The material, which is also used for some airplane wings, is very stiff and light. The frame of Armstrong's bike weighs just over 2 pounds. The wheels, pedals, and other components are also light. Having the lightest possible bike allows a rider to spend less energy pedaling and achieve higher speeds.

Few cyclists can match Lance Armstrong's feats. However, everyone who enjoys riding can share his love of the sport.

HOBBY HORSES AND BONESHAKERS

No one knows who invented the bicycle. Some people credit Leonardo da Vinci, an Italian artist and scientist. In the late 1400s, da Vinci is believed to have drawn a sketch of a machine with two wheels, handlebars, pedals, and a chain. However, no one in da Vinci's time actually built a bike.

About 300 years later, people in France and Germany made bicycle-like "hobby horses." These were similar to scooters, but with bigger wheels and seats. Hobby horses lacked pedals. Riders moved forward by pushing their feet along the ground.

Bicycle design began to make progress in the 1860s when inventors put pedals on bikes. This new machine was called a velocipede (vuh-LAH-suh-peed), meaning "fast foot."

The pedals on velocipedes gave riders a smoother forward motion, but the machines had problems. The pedals were attached to the center of the front wheel. Riders had to lean forward to pedal, throwing the bike off balance.

The wheel on a high wheeler was nearly as tall as the rider.

These early bikes were sometimes called boneshakers, for several reasons. The bikes' brakes didn't stop the machine; they just slowed it down. The frames and wheels were made of solid metal. That made for a bumpy ride, especially since roads were not paved.

The next design innovation was the high wheeler. This type of bike had a front wheel that could be up to 5 feet tall, with a seat perched over it. The back wheel was small. With one turn of the pedals, a high wheeler could move 15 feet.

High wheelers had hollow frames and solid rubber tires. These features made riding less bone-shaking.

The new bikes presented their own problems, though. Getting up to the seat was hard, even for tall riders. Stopping was also a challenge. If a rider braked too fast or too hard, the front wheel would stop and the rider would go flying over the handlebars. This headfirst fall became known as "taking a header."

Tricycles soon came along. Most had medium-sized back wheels and a smaller front wheel. Safer and more stable than earlier bikes, they brought the fun of cycling to children.

The "safety" bicycle, introduced in 1885, paved the way for modern bikes. It had two same-sized wheels. The rider could balance over the center of the bike and pedal straight downward. The pedals turned crank arms, which turned a chain. The chain powered the rear wheel and moved the bike forward. The same basic design is used for the bike we know today.

Biking is the most efficient type of travel ever invented. It takes less energy to bike a mile than to walk, ride a horse, or swim the same distance. Cars go faster than bikes, of course, but bikes don't require fuel as cars do. Bikes don't create pollution, which is one reason dedicated bike riders love them.

EVOLUTION OF THE BICYCLE

 Late 1700s Inventors build wooden hobby horses with no pedals.

 1860s Inventors create velocipedes, or boneshakers.

 1869 Inventors build high wheelers, with large front wheels and small back wheels.

 1885 The safety bicycle is introduced, using the same basic design as modern bikes.

 1888 John Boyd Dunlop patents the air-filled tire.

 1898 Inventors introduce coaster brakes (foot brakes).

 1970s Off-road bicyclists invent the first mountain bikes.

HOW BIKES WORK

A bicycle has a set of parts that work together. The most crucial part is not built in, though. That part is you—the rider. You're the engine that makes the bike go.

The frame holds the parts together. Some common materials used to make frames are steel, aluminum, titanium, and carbon fiber. There are reasons to select a bicycle frame made from each of these materials. For instance, steel is strong, but steel frames can be heavy. A heavy bike is harder to pedal. Titanium is much lighter, but it is also very expensive.

The steel-framed safety bicycle (left) weighed much more than a bike with a titanium frame.

Wheels and tires move the bike forward as the rider pedals. At the same time, they are subject to a force that slows down the bike. This force is called rolling resistance.

Resistance occurs when one thing works against another. In biking, the road surface resists forward motion. Rolling resistance is high on dirt roads and low on smooth pavement.

An important part of the bike is the transmission: the cranks, the pedals, and the chain. The bike's transmission also includes chain rings near the right crank and at the rear wheel hub. As the rider pedals, the chain goes around the chain rings and sends power to the back wheel. This action propels the bike forward.

Most bikes have more than one gear, or speed. An efficient rider needs to match the bike's gear to the terrain. Going uphill, riders use low gears to work against the force of gravity. On downhills and flat areas, riders use higher gears to go faster.

The gear-shifting devices are called derailleurs (duh-RAY-luhrs). These move, or "derail," the chain from ring to ring as the rider changes gears.

PARTS OF A BIKE

gear shifter

front derailleur

brake lever

brake cable

down tube   frame

rear brake pad

front brake pad

rim

fork

hub

crank   pedal

rear derailleur   chain   chain ring   spoke

Each time a rider changes gears, the derailleurs have the effect of making the chain longer or shorter. The chain is really still the same length. However, the rear derailleur takes up some of the chain, or lets it out, at the same time it is helping to move the chain from ring to ring.

How does this process work? Imagine measuring a length of rope from end to end, tying a loop in it, then measuring it again. The looped rope will be shorter than it was before.

The actual length, however, hasn't changed. In a similar way, the derailleur "loops" the chain and shortens it when you shift to a lower gear.

A shorter chain is easier to turn, so pedaling in a low gear helps you get up a hill with less effort. In contrast, shifting to a higher gear makes the chain longer. This makes the bike go farther forward with each turn of the pedals. You will cover more ground on easy terrain.

Some bikes have coaster brakes. The bikes slow down when you push backward on the pedals. This sets in motion a mechanism in the rear hub that stops the rear wheel only.

Most bikes use a type of brakes called calipers. Calipers are very efficient because they stop both wheels. You brake by squeezing both brake levers on the handlebar. Squeezing the levers pulls a set of cables, which presses the brake pads against the rims.

From a scientific view, the main problem in cycling is overcoming wind resistance, or drag. Racers and many road riders can do several things to reduce the effect of drag. For instance, they can use handlebars that curve downward, forcing riders to crouch down rather than sit upright.

Wearing tight-fitting clothing helps riders cut through the air more efficiently. They can also choose helmets designed to lower drag. In fact, the right helmet can even lower drag for a rider who is bald.

Human-powered vehicles (HPVs) are types of bicycles designed purely for speed, not for practical use. These HPVs are cycles inside sleek, bullet-shaped shells. Their riders sit low and pedal forward rather than downward. In 2002, HPV racer Sam Whittingham set the world record for human-powered speed at 81 miles per hour!

a human-powered vehicle

MOUNTAIN BIKING

Mountain bikes, or "fat-tire bikes," are America's best-selling bikes. They are designed for riding on dirt roads and in the woods, though people can ride them anywhere. They're sturdy and comfortable.

At first glance, mountain bikes seem like road bikes. However, they have heavier frames with shock-absorbing forks and seats. The frame has higher clearance from the ground. The tires are wider and are knobby, for good traction on trails. These features let riders travel more safely over rocks, roots, and bumpy terrain.

Mountain bikes are the best-selling bikes in America.

The brakes on mountain bikes are heavy-duty. The extra power helps riders control the bike when riding on slippery mud or down steep hills. Brake levers and gear levers are close to each other. That lets riders keep their hands on the bars at all times. Most mountain bikes also have very low gears for hill-climbing.

Off-road riders need good bike handling skills. Through practice, they learn to stay balanced as the terrain changes. To balance, riders shift their weight. They steer by leaning into a turn, not by turning the bars sharply. Even when riding safely, however, off-road riders can fall. Smart riders always wear helmets.

Mountain bike racing is a thrilling but dangerous sport. Racers rocket down slopes, jump their bikes over logs, and often crash.

One of the most famous mountain bike racers is Alison Dunlap. After competing in the 1996 Olympics as a road bicyclist, she began her professional mountain biking career.

Dunlap competed again in the 2000 Olympics, this time as a mountain bike rider. The next year, she won first place in the World Mountain Bike cross-country championships. Dunlap also won the 2002 World Cup title.

This determined athlete says she always took her father's advice: "Don't stop pedaling."

Racers aren't the only ones to do amazing things on mountain bikes. Riders have pedaled on snow to the top of Mount Kilimanjaro, Africa's tallest peak. They had fun going down!

Aside from sports, people around the world use wide-tired, heavy-duty bikes for daily tasks. For example, almost 300 million people in China have bikes, but only 3 million have cars. Like people in many Asian countries, they use bikes to get to work, to go to school, and to shop. In America, though, fat-tire bikes are mainly a great way to have fun.

In China, bicycles are a common sight in traffic.

17

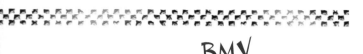

BMX

Take the fun of biking, add the thrill of racing, and throw in the gravity-defying moves of skateboarding. The result is BMX, which stands for bicycle motocross.

BMX is really two sports. There is BMX racing, done on dirt tracks with banked turns and mounds for jumping. There is also BMX freestyle, or stunt riding. This sport is done on special courses with wooden ramps and railings.

Bikes for both types of BMX have small frames, wide tires, upturned handlebars, and one gear. BMX racing bikes are fairly light, for maximum speed. BMX freestyle bikes are heavier, for maximum strength, and have pegs on the wheel axles for added balance.

BMX racing is a family-friendly sport. In official competitions, riders are grouped by age and skill level. You might see a boy riding in the age six **novice** division and his sister in the age ten intermediate division. Their brother might be an expert in a teenage division. Their parents would compete in the adult group.

Dave Mirra landed his double backflip at the 2000 X Games in San Francisco.

Most BMX races last less than a minute. Riders sprint out of the starting gate and go just once around the track. The winner is the one who maneuvers the obstacles and finishes first. The best riders ride smoothly, not just quickly.

Freestyle competitors have to do a certain number of stunts within a set time. They jump railings, do backflips, and turn in the air. These moves take great balance—and a lot of practice.

One BMX pro, Dave "Miracle Boy" Mirra, competed for 16 years before doing the first-ever double backflip in competition. Mirra has won numerous gold medals at X Games, Gravity Games, and other competitions.

COMPARING TYPES OF BIKES

Type of Bike	Frame	Tires	Gears (Speeds)	Handlebars
Mountain	Rugged	Wide	At least 21	Straight
BMX	Rugged	Wide	1	Upturned
Road Racing	Ultralight	Narrow	16 to 18	Dropped
Track Racing	Ultralight	Narrow	1	Dropped
Road	Light	Medium	10 to 30	Dropped or straight

Safety measures are enforced at all official BMX events. Bikes must have padding on the handlebars, handlebar stem, and top tube. Riders must wear a helmet, long pants, and a long-sleeved shirt. Many also choose to wear knee pads, elbow pads, shin guards, and gloves.

Good BMX riders know a lot about balance, safety, and nerve. If you are athletic and competitive, BMX can be a great choice. If you're interested in the sport, you can check out the clinics for beginners at BMX tracks around the United States. They'll help you develop better skills.

RACING AND LONG-DISTANCE RIDING

Bike racing comes in many forms. What all racers share is their love of competition.

Road racers such as Lance Armstrong usually get into the sport through short races. They start as novices and move up as they build their racing skills.

To improve, racers often train and ride on teams. They practice pacelining, or cycling in a line of riders. Also called drafting, pacelining involves leading a chain of riders for a time, then rotating to the back of the line.

Pacelines are very aerodynamic. The group cuts through wind resistance faster than a single rider can. In long races, including the Tour de France, teams use pacelines to keep a steady speed. Then, their lead riders break away. Drafting helps them save energy for the sprints that may decide the race.

Your local community can offer exciting road races. If you live in a city, look for races called criteriums. Racing organizations sponsor these. There are races for children and adults.

Short courses wind through streets and parks. The course is closed to cars during the race. In a 60-mile criterium, the course might be 2 miles long, and the riders would "lap" it 30 times.

Standing on the sidewalks, spectators can watch the drama unfold. Colorfully clad racers will swerve around corners, fight for position, and chase each other to the finish.

Another form of competitive racing takes place indoors, on tracks called velodromes. Cyclists compete on a circular track with banked sides. These contests of skill thrill participants and audiences alike.

Bikes built for track racing have no brakes and only one gear. The bike's speed is controlled entirely by the rider's pedaling. In some track races, riders compete alone, racing against the clock in time trials. In this type of race, cyclists go as fast as they can, pushing themselves to the limits of their endurance.

Other riders compete against each other or race in teams. They can race distances as short as 1 kilometer (about 6/10 of a mile) or as long as 40 kilometers (about 25 miles).

You don't need to race to cover distances.

Organized touring rides make fun family vacations.

Every summer, casual riders make organized touring rides across whole states. They pedal at their own pace. At night, they camp and socialize. Cross-state tours are friendly events. They make fun family vacations.

One of the best things about biking is that it is a lifetime sport. Also, it offers plenty of styles of riding and types of bikes. You can find the bike and the style that suits you. Best of all, as a bike rider, you'll always enjoy the great feeling of going places under your own power.

GLOSSARY

aerodynamic   referring to the interaction of air and moving objects

calipers   brakes that work by pressing against the sides of a wheel

clinic   a workshop or class

composite   a material made up of two or more different substances

efficient   productive without causing waste

innovation   something new

novice   a person new to an activity; a beginner

resistance   an opposing force

spectators   people who watch an event

terrain   an area of land and its natural features

traction   friction or grip

transmission   an assembly of parts that includes speed-changing gears

velodromes   oval tracks built for bicycle racing